TIME RICH EMPIRE

TIME RICH EMPIRE

"Wealth Freedom, Self Ownership, How-to Make Money In Your Spare Time Building Passive Income Secrets"

By

KYLE RANSOM

Dedications

All my family members and closest friends... Beautiful wife and daughter!

All content ©Copyright material and published by Uply Media, Inc 2018. All rights reserved. This material can not be reproduced without permission.

TIME RICH EMPIRE

Contents

Intro   Why Time Rich Empire Is For You?

Session 1 Mental Marathon

Session 2 Understanding Passive Income

Session 3 How-to Create Passive Income Blogs That Make 10k & Up Monthly

Session 4 Simple Passive Income Ideas To Start With Little Money In Your Spare Time

Session 5 Promote Yourself Like A Passive Income Rock Star To Make More Money

TIME RICH EMPIRE

Introduction

The most valuable asset on earth right now is time and being in control over your time is the path to wealth freedom.

Ask yourself this one question, "could you be anywhere in the world right now and stay for an extended time-frame?"

Likely, the true answer to that question is "no" because most people do have time responsibilities to others.

In their quest for wealth individuals are "clueless" that time is their best asset. Unless people understand that building wealth is connected to controlling their time, finding true happiness will always be an issue.

Without control over your time, self-ownership belongs to someone else and not you.

After crude oil coffee is considered the second most-traded commodity in the world. Now take this same theory and apply drinking coffee to the value of time.

People spend hours in coffee shops just drinking coffee. "Why?"

TIME RICH EMPIRE

It's an enjoyable way to spend their time.

Discover simple techniques to build passive income around time experiences.

"This is how to truly build a passive rich lifestyle!"

Cheers to your success.

Why Is Time Rich Empire For You?

In my in-depth research to find wealth freedom, I discovered that the number one illiteracy was visual.

"It's a scary fact that people can't interpret visual perception."

I observed that everyone who was trying to create wealth, operated like a "social influencer robot" all visually looking the same.

An assembly line of like and similar individuals all doing the exact same thing, even if their focus was a different niche or industry.

"Visually most people can't interpret different

TIME RICH EMPIRE

perceptions."

This leads to one failed business venture after the next and always slaving to find the next grand hustle.

Building a "Time Rich Empire" is actually a much smarter and sustainable hustle.

It's just that most people don't understand how-to build a passive income lifestyle.

First, understand that your business should not be built for social media. Typically, most people simply don't understand that concept either.

Social media should be for engagement and utilized as a platform for brand awareness...nothing more.

If you want to have wealth freedom to do whatever you want, "passive income" is the fastest solution to achieve this goal.

Time Rich Empire is for you if want to discover a faster way to make serious money and without having to work hard to do so. Even if you attempted to make money with passive income before and failed, now is your time to take control and turn things around to make a

TIME RICH EMPIRE

profitable living.

"Are you still drinking the social media Kool-Aid, that advertising on social media will explode your business and vastly generate more revenue?"

If that was true, we would all be generating mass revenue online just by "advertising" inside social media platforms.

If you understood the theory of how data works, then you could better understand that social media produces a ROI (return on investment) for engagement and credibility with nothing more than just that, social media is not intended to drive online revenue.

While engagement and influential credibility can assist to encourage someone to trust your brand's trustworthiness...there are still important missing sectors being ignored on a larger scale to influence buying power.

Despite all the claims that social media influencers drive immense online traffic to websites "leaving you to visually believe the image that social media ads work to increase online sales."

While the relevance of powerful social media platforms do count.

TIME RICH EMPIRE

Today's businesses are overwhelmingly overlooking a dynamic core platform concentration to "target open web browsing" where 70% of the time is being spent by consumers.

Learning the methods for how theory guides research to create a "Time Rich Empire" online using data science is the best way to build a passive income lifestyle.

"After all wouldn't it just make sense to open up a business model where most people are spending 70% of their time, browsing the web for things online?"

If you haven't put it together by now "Time Rich Empire" is about creating passive income from profitable resources, that will allow you to have self ownership over your time.

Not making an investment in someone else, only investing in yourself to build a passive income rich lifestyle.

The only way to control your time is to take control over who owns it.

To achieve this you must be the boss and have 100% total control, not buying into "be your own boss" while working for a company not owned by you and promoting you work for yourself.

TIME RICH EMPIRE

Mental Marathon

How you condition and train your mental thinking will deeply determine successes. This is a mental marathon and you must train to achieve your goals to make it happen. It's no different than training for a marathon race or sports training.

First off, you should want wealth freedom for the right reasons. So ask yourself "what are my reasons for wanting wealth freedom?"

I can tell you this "fear factor" is why most people don't mentally succeed.

If you want to build a Time Rich Empire, understand that you will need to invent your own online concepts and business ideas.

Determine right now what your work ethics and techniques are going to be. Without a strong work ethic or discipline, you will not be able to pull it off.

Running a business is stressful, this means you must stay fit and healthy, plus mentally healthy as well.

Albert Einstein said that "If you want to live a happy life, tie it to a goal, not to people or objects."

TIME RICH EMPIRE

Only you hold the power to believe in yourself. So in order to start believing in yourself truly, it takes understanding what controls motivation. "How this works" is that dopamine is a chemical in the brain strongly associated with motivation. If you focus your self-belief this causes a wide surge of dopamine.

To motivate yourself requires vision to focus on a positive self-image of yourself. This is where you form an inner strength and ability to believe in yourself and your ability to be successful at all times.

"Do you crack under pressure or find it difficult to handle new challenges?"

The root for this problem is to build a belief DNA identity in yourself. Create supernatural powers to see yourself achieving goals. This will build motivation to be successful through an organic DNA belief.

Another key factor is to "only surround yourself" around other positive individuals who also believe in you as well.

Receiving positive feedback from others about your ability to do well, also helps to release dopamine too.

TIME RICH EMPIRE

To get mentally motivated requires controlled enthusiasm. I once heard Tony Robbins express that he has the ability to make himself happy everyday.

I believe that this is totally a trained act and one that can be mentally controlled. To do this you have to be able to develop a mindset for concentrated prosperity, expecting to receive immense abundance and giving through generosity. Oppose to hoping to receive and not wanting to share resources with others.

Practicing motivation skills helps to strength a circuit in the brain. Why this works is that when uncertainty comes, practicing motivation will help to be ready and prepared.

Only you have the ability inside to "create a mental strategy" to achieve your goals. However, it takes empowering your business mind for success. Before you can be effective, starts by first not feeling powerless over everything you seek to accomplish.

Internal belief is the engine that drives success. There will always be challenging situations that bring on stress, change, and uncertainty. It's up to you to build a mental strategy or have one in place to be resilient toward challenges. This is the predictor of

TIME RICH EMPIRE

successful outcome or failure by feeling powerless to challenges.

"Emotional awareness" is the key element to handle every challenge that comes your way. Many psychological experts believe in order to achieve this mental ability involves looking inside yourself and examining your thoughts and emotions. The introspective concept of taking an existential view of yourself. This will improve your mental ability to function at optimal levels on the path to becoming very successful.

When you have a built-in emotional awareness, it drives your self-awareness to be brave and even think independently. Producing the ability to rely exclusively on your own mental state of mind to succeed. Without having a sound business mind to believe in yourself, "it is impossible to be successful" in challenging times.

Belief requires commitment on your part, you can't just say "I believe in myself" to be successful. Firm belief requires setting a mental recharge to handle any doubt or delay. I have always viewed a delay as a test of patience and not a setback. You can never allow any delay to be driven by doubt, this thought will kill your success.

TIME RICH EMPIRE

Take action "results are produced by action" to achieve success. You must know deep down that you are fearless, bold, and determined to be successful.

"I have found having no fear of loss in business" to be my greatest asset. I am determined and driven to be successful. However, my fearlessness is an asset I hold true to my character and personality to achieve every business goal I set for myself.

Never forget to be mindful also of all circumstances and situations. Make it a point to give attention by listening to others. Before you make any decisions or form opinions always gather pertinent information.

Stephen Richards Covey's "The 7 Habits of Highly Effective People." Habit 5: Seek First to Understand, Then to Be Understood.

Mindfulness trains you to pay attention to detail and not neglect any areas of your business. Always be mindful and emotionally aware of what's going on around you will be important on your path to success.

Understanding Passive Income

To better understand passive income, first, you need to understand key elements that makeup passive income.

To have passive income means to receive a cash flow on a regular basis. At the same time, this receiving of cash flow must require minimal to little effort on your part to maintain. Hence the "passive income" lifestyle. This is why people would buy into a 4 Hour work week or building real estate riches with zero down.

Income is categorized into three broad types:

Active income, passive income, and portfolio income.

Keep in mind the best passive income examples will always require, just minimal to little effort on your part to maintain.

Simple passive income strategies involve:

- Any type of cash flowing from property income.
- Profits, cash flow, and earnings from any business that does not require direct involvement from the owner or merchant;
- Rental income and incoming cash flow from a property or any piece of real estate.

- Interest income derived from any bank account or pension.
- Royalties paid from intellectual property such as music, books, manuscripts, computer software, or a patent;
- Earnings from internet advertisements on a website; blogs make great passive income.
- Dividend and interest income in the form of cash flow or capital gains from owning securities and commodities, such as stocks, currencies, gold, silver, ETFs, and bonds, is usually referred to as portfolio income, which may or is not considered a form of passive income.

In the United States, portfolio income is considered to be a different type of income than passive income.

How I built my "passive income" was by chance of some really bad luck as a result of the mortgage crisis that occurred in the United States. However, I learned to take lemons and turn them into lemonade by creating my own career guide for personal happiness and growth.

Most people often find themselves stuck between seeking a new job, changing careers, or returning to work from a career break. This should also be why everyone must always be willing to learn new skills, advance in

TIME RICH EMPIRE

personal growth, and sharpen professional development skills to advance.

"So why not create a career guide path for yourself using passive income revenue streams?"

First off, if I had to create a passive income revenue stream right now today...I would think outside of the box and likely not start some of the same income streams that operate as passive income for me today. We own and operate several websites that are over 10 and 11 years old. Many of them would likely not make it as profitable passive income streams if they were started from scratch today.

The best ways to make money in your spare time from passive income streams today would be creating online hubs that help people solve problems. That might sound too simple, but this is the fastest way to make money through passive income revenue streams. Which can make you super rich with little to no effort at the same time.

"After learning how-to create passive income revenue streams I was 100% sold."

I did mention that I discovered how to make money in passive income by chance of really bad luck. From 2007-2010, the U.S. subprime mortgage crisis became a nationwide banking emergency. This put the state of the economy in

TIME RICH EMPIRE

a standstill recession from December 2007 - June of 2009. Which resulted in a large decline in home prices after the housing bubble collapsed. Many people found themselves in foreclosure situations, mortgage defaults were on the rise, and devaluation of housing-related securities was a big problem across the nation.

Not to mention the thriving mortgage business that I had built for the last 15 years, as a top mortgage broker to real estate investors went belly up. My real estate investments were tanked and I was no longer able to fund my land development deals.

"Things were really bad for my family, we lost everything."

After constantly feeling defeated, losing totally everything. Having absolutely no money in my bank account. Being so broke that I couldn't even figure out one single solution to make any money.

It never occurred to me then that I should have been trying to figure out how to make money in my spare time, without having to work so hard for it. See over 11 years ago, I had no clue exactly what passive income truly meant or even how to make money from this way of thinking.

All I knew was that I had no more real estate left, no assets and no net worth.

TIME RICH EMPIRE

personal growth, and sharpen professional development skills to advance.

"So why not create a career guide path for yourself using passive income revenue streams?"

First off, if I had to create a passive income revenue stream right now today...I would think outside of the box and likely not start some of the same income streams that operate as passive income for me today. We own and operate several websites that are over 10 and 11 years old. Many of them would likely not make it as profitable passive income streams if they were started from scratch today.

The best ways to make money in your spare time from passive income streams today would be creating online hubs that help people solve problems. That might sound too simple, but this is the fastest way to make money through passive income revenue streams. Which can make you super rich with little to no effort at the same time.

"After learning how-to create passive income revenue streams I was 100% sold."

I did mention that I discovered how to make money in passive income by chance of really bad luck. From 2007-2010, the U.S. subprime mortgage crisis became a nationwide banking emergency. This put the state of the economy in

TIME RICH EMPIRE

a standstill recession from December 2007 - June of 2009. Which resulted in a large decline in home prices after the housing bubble collapsed. Many people found themselves in foreclosure situations, mortgage defaults were on the rise, and devaluation of housing-related securities was a big problem across the nation.

Not to mention the thriving mortgage business that I had built for the last 15 years, as a top mortgage broker to real estate investors went belly up. My real estate investments were tanked and I was no longer able to fund my land development deals.

"Things were really bad for my family, we lost everything."

After constantly feeling defeated, losing totally everything. Having absolutely no money in my bank account. Being so broke that I couldn't even figure out one single solution to make any money.

It never occurred to me then that I should have been trying to figure out how to make money in my spare time, without having to work so hard for it. See over 11 years ago, I had no clue exactly what passive income truly meant or even how to make money from this way of thinking.

All I knew was that I had no more real estate left, no assets and no net worth.

TIME RICH EMPIRE

"Talk about feeling worthless, I went from wealthy to totally flat broke."

This is when I learned about people fixing up websites, making them profitable, and flipping websites. At that moment I just needed to feel like I could own something of value.

A website domain name was fairly cheap to buy, you could purchase one for $15 to $30 a year during that time. So I purchased as many as I could afford to buy and got a loan from my father-in-law and a few trusted friends who were going broke too. Believe me, just finding someone during this time to loan me even $15 to $30 was almost impossible. During the recession, everyone I knew was going through almost some sort of financial crisis.

It also didn't help that most of my business associates made their money from the real estate industry. They had actually lost everything like I did. Times were really bad.

My first website real estate development project was https://TopAtlantaLuxury.com/, launched in 2007 today this site is a website portal for Atlanta luxury experiences. We developed this project to profit from metro Atlanta's luxury lifestyle, my wife and I operate as business partners. She had lots of knowledge about the luxury industry and did public relations for luxury brands.

TIME RICH EMPIRE

Most of her clients during the recession were also real estate investors or developers, so when their businesses went under so did a huge portion of her business. We would be starting in this new business venture together and having no knowledge of online business or passive income.

Lucky for us luxury brands needed websites to promote products and services. However, we didn't know where to start to get advertisers interested in promoting products and services on our site.

Thinking old school, we cranked out a Flyer and hit local shopping centers. All we got were quick and fast "no" because people were just not interested in online advertising. Back then typically it was not uncommon to encounter businesses that didn't even have their own company website. Which would also make sense to decline to advertise on our site?

It seemed like nothing was working, we didn't have money to cover our basic living expenses. There was no money for food or anything else. No rich friends or relatives either, we had borrowed our last dime.

"I remember the day our refrigerator was empty. There was nothing inside that we hadn't eaten, even if it was bad food."

TIME RICH EMPIRE

Reaching my breaking point of seeing my family struggling, I declared that I would turn things around. Earlier that day I had received a phone call from a former real estate investor client. The bank was giving him a really hard time and forcing him into foreclosure.

I mapped out a mortgage securitization audit solution to find errors with the mortgage loan.

"It worked, he saved his home from foreclosure!"

This was how I discovered that creating online hubs to help people solve problems is the best way to make passive income revenue streams. My wife and I started brainstorming about what solutions we could offer through online websites.

We both agreed that our purpose for https://TopAtlantaLuxury.com/ needed to be about more than just highlighting Atlanta luxury lifestyle. How solving problems for advertisers would be the perfect solution to make the site profitable.

If we provided information for Atlanta luxury experiences, we could connect people to more luxury businesses in the metro Atlanta area. Allowing us to build one of metro Atlanta's top website portals for Atlanta luxury experiences. Today our site is a specialty local expert

TIME RICH EMPIRE

guide on luxury experiences in metro Atlanta, GA.

After discovering how-to make passive income through advertisers and sponsored content on Top Atlanta Luxury, our next move was to re-evaluate all of our websites.

Prior to 2007, we operated https://MosnarCommunications.com/ to promote my wife's luxury PR services. Which we grew into a very profitable business until the recession hit. Taking what we learned from our success with https://TopAtlantaLuxury.com/ we duplicated this same concept with MC and it worked again.

Next, we turned CharmPosh.com named for our daughter Charm into a kids lifestyle blog of posh things. Including kids fashion and all things family travel and lifestyle. Once again, we scored more success with creating passive income through our websites.

However, if I had to create new passive income revenue streams today, these types of sites would not be the best way to go. I say this because making 10k a month from a blog is much easier than most people think. Most people are trying to either make money as a social media influencer or blogger.

Which they have their concepts set up all wrong. It's a smarter idea to create passive

TIME RICH EMPIRE

income revenue streams that you can do in your spare time and are profitable over what you might have a passion to do.

"Yes, that goes against everything that so-called gurus are teaching."

What I found interesting is that many gurus really don't have businesses focused on industries what they teach. However, they attempt to coach you how-to-succeed in various business industries that they are not also operating in. Yet, the guru is no longer operating their businesses in certain industries or must partner with someone who is leading in a particular industry to look successful.

"Things to make you go hmmm, right?"

Since theory guides research, this little discovery focused me in the right direction. All the gurus are focused on trying to help people solve problems.

"What if we could create products that help people solve problems??"

That would make us "time rich," especially if we developed these products as passive income revenue streams. Stay tuned, I'm about to lay it all out in this next session ahead.

TIME RICH EMPIRE
How-to Create Passive Income Blogs That Make 10k & Up Monthly

Creating passive income blogs in your spare time and making 10k a month from one single blog is much easier than most people would think.

"This information is not too good to be true, this is the real deal and you deserve to learn skills for creating your own destiny to becoming time rich."

In my introduction, I explained why Time Rich Empire is designed for you. The mere fact that you have continued on with reading and studying this material, tells me that Time Rich Empire offers the exact solutions that you have been seeking. To sum it all up, Time Rich Empire is about to solve all your problems for how-to create passive income in your spare time with little effort to make it happen.

After I show you the skills and technique to create your first blog making 10k or more a month, "I imagine you will be sold?"

What this does is make our relationship a win-win and builds trust between us. I trust that you will take this information and execute it properly to become successful. In a sense, we are partnering to help you establish wealth freedom and self-ownership using the strategies

TIME RICH EMPIRE

of my expertise to make money in your spare time building passive income secrets.

The more successful you become attaches to Time Rich Empire building more credibility and influential value.

Now that we have gotten the purpose for why I want to help you out the way, let's get down to serious business. One of the most cost-effective ways, requiring very little money to get started and affordable solutions to build passive income revenue streams in your spare time is blogging. You seriously don't need much money to get started and can turn 10k or more a month fast if you implement the right strategies.

Think of your blog as an online real estate development project and yourself as a savvy business entrepreneur. I don't think of our sites as blogs, they are online information platforms. We are publishers connecting people to best resources, services, and products that solve all their problems.

I just revealed the best way to make as much as 10k or more a month from blogging. To do this all you need to do is create an online hub, which is your "blog" that connects people to best resources, services, and products that will solve all their problems.

TIME RICH EMPIRE

I recall making over $4,500 from one single blog post in one month with Google Adsense. During that same month, that same blog made over $1,200 in one day from just Google Adsense alone. Despite what people tell you, this is still very possible. You can still make tons of money with Google Adsense by connecting people to information that provide best solutions and answers to their problems.

"Are you still wondering what type of blog post could generate over $4,500 in one month and over $1,200 in one single day?"

Well, I will share with you that actual blog post went on to continue to generate as much as $1,200 dollars a month for several years. Requiring me to do absolutely nothing other than promoting my knowledge in this expertise and directing people to the blog posts every now and then.

However, things are a little different today. Which because of the popularity of social media, you can create this same type of passive income revenue stream and work less. While still being able to produce the same results.

"Are you still dying of suspense about what type of blog post produced this type of crazy

TIME RICH EMPIRE

money making passive income monthly revenue stream?"

It was a very simple blog post during the Subprime mortgage crisis resulting in the Great Recession, that told people where to get "foreclosure help" from the U.S. Government if they were unemployed. Following the Subprime mortgage crisis occurring between 2007 - 2010, lots of businesses went under and many homeowners were left out of work and unemployed. They had no way to pay their mortgage notes, so learning about free help from the U.S. Government to pay their mortgages was a solution to all their problems.

Google Adsense was paying top dollar for foreclosure help keywords during that time. Which lasted for several years until the economy restored back to health. Some people still don't believe that the recession hasn't ended. However, those specific programs designed to help unemployed homeowners with mortgages to prevent foreclosures ended.

From that experience, it taught me to focus on creating passive income revenue streams that would be sustainable (never ending) and in evergreen niches. This is what I am going to break down for you and explain how easy it is to create blogs that make 10k or more a month as passive income.

TIME RICH EMPIRE

Before you ever decide which blogging platform to build your blog on. The first thing you must do is to determine what your blog will be about and how you plan to monetize to make money from your blog.

Once you determine the niche of your blog, then design elements can be decided after you know what the blog will be about.

Selecting a niche that is profitable is the ultimate way to make 10k or more a month from your blog. Remember, I already said to not focus on passion but concentrate on niches that make money.

This is going to be a passive income revenue stream, generating enough time and money for you to do what you are passionate about. For this project, it's about thinking like a true entrepreneur building an online publishing empire.

Once you select a profitable niche, then your blog will set out to solve problems for people in that niche. Be creative about offering your own informational products, ebooks, resources, affiliate partnerships, etc.

The more ownership you control for offers, allows you to have influential value in the niche. Your blog should offer the best

TIME RICH EMPIRE

resources, services, and products in your niche, which increases the number of revenue streams you will make as passive income.

What's a good example of a blog or how-to determine the type of niche that can generate 10k or more a month?

This requires you to think like a serious entrepreneur before you launch your first blog. Conduct some research before you ever set up your blog.

"I love to drink coffee and know that other people also love to drink coffee."

Enjoying drinking coffee made me want to conduct some research on this niche. One thing I noticed was that coffee shops don't go out of business much. I thought it would be good to create passive income revenue streams from coffee lovers.

In order to do that, first I needed to explore if a niche about coffee was even worth my time. Turns out after a quick search in Google's keyword finder "coffee" was an awesome niche with excellent search traffic and good paying keyword revenue for clicks.

Here is something that I always caution, never build a blog for Google Adsense. Always build a

TIME RICH EMPIRE

blog to help people solve problems in a profitable niche. Think like this and you can generate 10k or more per month blogs over and over every time.

We launched eCoffeeFinder.com as a coffee media and entertainment digital promotional platform. The site receives financial contributions through affiliate and sponsored advertising partners.

Allowing passive income revenue streams that require, just minimal to little effort on our part to maintain.

Coffee is worth over $100 billion dollars worldwide and working with eCoffeeFinder presents dynamic digital advertising solutions to connect with Coffee lovers around the world. The global Coffee industry export alone is worth $20 billion dollars. After crude oil Coffee is the most sought-after commodity in the world.

I have found that the best way to make the most money from blogging is to include your own information product offering also with your blog's niche focus.

Offer an information product that resolves how-to solve a problem focused on the profitable niche of your blog.

TIME RICH EMPIRE

Creating a series of information products ranging from $79 to $1,250 is ideal. Set goals for the number of information products you want to sell per month. Which will put you on a fast path to making 10k or more per month from your blog.

To be successful requires starting blogs in profitable niches. In order for the niche to be profitable, requires that people are searching for the niche topic. Generally, you should be targeting profitable niches with searches over 100,000 or above monthly. Don't worry about high competition, you have a strategy to attract people interested in the profitable niche by solving all their problems.

Passive income revenue streams are considered low hanging fruit opportunities to make money. However, it should always require minimal to little effort on your part to maintain.

Visit https://timerichempire.com, to sign up for Time Rich Empire Newsletter which reveals how-to setup profitable passive income revenue streams all in your spare time and more. Get all the details and necessary tools monthly for free to make your Time Rich Empire action plan super successful. If you are serious about building a Time Rich Empire you will need these super secrets.

TIME RICH EMPIRE

Simple Passive Income Ideas To Start With Little Money In Your Spare Time

You will want to create passive income ideas that you can actually start with little money as possible. Now that you fully understand what passive income truly is, let's explore some very simple business ideas you can start to generate fast and quick passive income revenue streams.

Earlier I mentioned, <u>Time Rich Empire Passive Income Newsletter</u>, this is my monthly free newsletter that explores how-to setup profitable passive income revenue streams all in your spare time and more. Every month my team and I explore the best passive income revenue streams that are the most profitable and show you step-by-step how to get started. Which is why it truly makes sense to sign up for this free information and if you serious about creating passive income revenue streams.

For now, I want to introduce you to simple passive income ideas to start with little money in your spare time.

Ebook Author - Writing an ebook is a great passive income revenue earning strategy. Every time that you sell a book allows residual income. The earning potential of being an ebook author is limitless.

TIME RICH EMPIRE

Amazon Kindle is the big player in the ebook marketplace, their market share accounts for 83% of all ebook purchases sold in the United States. The other ebooks sold are shared by Apple's iBookStore, Barnes & Noble, Kobo U.S. and GooglePlay books.

Lead Generation Site - Create a site around a specific niche and generate leads for local businesses.

Blogging - Create a blog that solves problems for others by offering passive income revenue streams. Sell information products, including affiliate services and resources that pay you.

Review and Comparison Site - Build a site dedicated to reviews and comparison of goods, services, and products for a specific niche that solve problems for others. Generate passive income from advertisers and selling information products or affiliate services.

Professional Legal Kits - Scale the need for professional legal services. Partner with law offices and attorneys by having them create the professional legal form templates. Operate as the publisher of the professional legal forms like divorce kits, will/ estate kits, credit repair kits, etc.

Professional Training Kits - Scale the need for professional training services. Partner with

TIME RICH EMPIRE

individuals with professional licenses to create training material. Operate as the publisher of the professional niche training guides and practices.

Peer-To-Peer Lending - Grow your passive income revenue stream by investing in peer to peer lending. Prosper will allow you to invest with as little as $25 to get started.

Manufacture Products - Create a product that solves a problem in an industry. Manufacture a product that will solve a problem for the specific niche industry.

Buy Domain Names - Purchase domain names to buy, hold or flip for a profit. Make sure the domain name is related to a niche that is also a popular search term that is a sustainable evergreen subject matter.

Buy Online Business - Purchase an affordable online business that is operating a passive income revenue stream and would require little effort from you to maintain.

Space Share Renting - Rent out space, spare room, etc. Get creative by promoting and marketing other space share renting available for a fee.

Information Products - Create information products that solve problems for other people. Research problems and gain an expert knowledge or partner with someone with expertise to

TIME RICH EMPIRE

create information products to sell online for a profit.

Membership Sites - Bring people with a similar interest together by providing a membership site that solves their problems. Charge a fee for online membership access.

Consumer Review Videos - Develop consumer review videos to put on sites like YouTube to make ad revenue.

Keep in mind you should seek to only start passive income ideas that cost little money down to get started and require little to no effort on your part to maintain. Make this your strategy to make passive income across the board and you will make lots of money with small investments to get started.

The one thing you will need to have is a website. Your website is your information hub that connects people together and provide instructions for how-to best communicate with you.

p.S. Please don't forget to sign up for **Time Rich Empire Passive Income Newsletter**, receive free tips and advice to grow passive income revenue in your spare time and more. Also, I Created a special welcome package of best software and resources I use to make to my passive income businesses run smoothly and profitable.

TIME RICH EMPIRE
Promote Yourself Like A Passive Income Rock Star To Make More Money

People always ask us, "what is it that you do, exactly?"do you work for a company that pays you, are you self-employed??

Which are all fair questions, I do have control over my time and people who see this often wonder how I can afford this lifestyle. To not confuse you, building a passive income business or any business requires that you put time and effort into the business before reaping success.

One passive income story that I am most inspired by is Pat Flynn's passive income success.

The way his story is delivered in the media is similar to a passive income rock star. It's asserted that he actually started out making only $38,000 a year in 2007, working with his architecture license. When he learned about Leadership in Energy and Environmental Design (LEED), this prompted him to explore taking a challenging exam to receive a credential in sustainable design and environmentally friendly building.

As a result, Flynn created a blog that focused on preparing for the exam. Which could allow

TIME RICH EMPIRE

him to participate with others in forums online to discuss strategies to pass the exam. Solving his own problem by creating the blog, Pat is rumored to have aced the exam and got a big promotion to $60,000.

However, the economy was slowing down because of the financial crisis, he was later laid off from his job. At the same time, just as Pat's blog solved his problem for how to pass the exam, it was also still solving other people's problems interested in the same thing and receiving thousands of visitors daily.

Through this experience, Pat later created an exam study guide ebook for $19.99, estimated to have earned $7,905.55 from passive income that same month. Later in 2008, he started his blog called Smart Passive Income and joined the passive income rock star elite. He is also most known for sharing passive income earnings break down and is a famous Podcaster on the subject matter.

One thing I noticed, in particular, is that if you want to make money or more money, "promote yourself like an expert" to attract a tribe. This is essential to achieve success and what all celebrities and rock stars do. They make it so that people want to be affiliated with them or even seen out with them.

Most people feel like they don't know where to start when it comes to self-promotions. To

TIME RICH EMPIRE

create passive income requires that you have some expertise on the subject matter or access to experts.

This is my guide for setting yourself up as a passive income rock star to stand out in the crowd.

"Create Your Hub"

Everything you do should first start with a hub, "your website" the central location where you build content and control communications. This is the platform to connect your expertise for your passive income streams. What I also like about creating a hub from a website platform, is that you get to connect social media channels to engage and promote your hub.

Make sure to set goals, brainstorm and stick to a serious schedule. I remember attending a conference where the speaker confessed to having the "exact same" daily routine that he practiced every single day for one year.

For instance, he had the same breakfast, lunch, and dinner for an entire year. "For me, this might be a little too drastic, I get bored easily and like to experience new and exciting things all the time."

Although for the speaker it worked out, this practice forced him to focus on his passive income business every day at the same time like clockwork. While it is still important to set

TIME RICH EMPIRE

goals and schedules, especially brainstorming times. Create a solution that will work for you and not disrupt your quality of life by doing so.

"Brand Your Image"

As a passive income expert, you must make sure that you brand your image to represent the persona of the brand to connect with target audiences.

That means creating a brand image or logo helping others to identify your brand's concept. Establish a soundbite that represents your passive income expertise. Always focus on consistency to help increase brand awareness.

If you change up your brand's fonts, colors, and the message it can confuse your target audience.

"Resonate Your Story"

To be a passive income rock star, resonating your story with your target audiences is what works best. That way each time you begin a passive income revenue stream, your audience is connected to you as the expert and understand that you establish only trustworthy businesses.

I have launched many different successful websites, so when I back another website my target audiences already trust the integrity and quality that always go into each of my passive income projects. This is because I am constantly communicating with them from my hub, expressing new interests in topics.

Having a hub also gives me an insider advantage to let my audiences know that I truly care and a better way to gain insider advantage for exploring passive income solutions to help them solve problems.

Again, a "win-win" helping people solve problems and creating passive income possibilities by solving more problems faster.

"Network, Network, Network"

Networking is a huge part of building your passive income success. By networking, you can establish mutually beneficial relationships with others focused on building passive income. Networking allows you to build business relationships and also attract potential clients or customers to your passive income business.

When you actively network, it allows you to tell others about your passive income business and can help turn them into potential customers. Being visible at networking events is the perfect way to create brand awareness and build a rock star reputation around your expertise.

TIME RICH EMPIRE

Hurry, don't forget to visit https://timerichempire.com, to sign up for **Time Rich Empire Newsletter** which reveals how-to setup profitable passive income revenue streams all in your spare time.

Best of luck and to your success.

Cheers,

Kyle Ransom

p.s. I've been thinking about the deal we made. Your success is important to me, so I have something else to share. Continue on.........

TIME RICH EMPIRE

IF YOU COULD INCREASE YOUR PASSIVE INCOME EARNINGS 50X AND BUILD WEALTH FREEDOM, WOULD HAVING MORE TIME ENRICH YOUR LIFE?

Time Rich Empire - Passive Income Secrets "Step-by-Step Scale Funnel System" Guide To Increase Earnings 50X offers tested systems to satisfy helping you reach your profit potential!

I want to give you my complete scale funnel system to help you grow and have a chance to increase your earnings 50X by learning the secret techniques used in my system.

These are the same techniques I have used to grow my media company Uply Media, Inc into a multi million-dollar brand.

Uply Media, Inc's revenue can be verified by Owler.

https://www.owler.com/company/uplymedia

I'm not trying to sell you on the success of my brands, "I myself hate it when gurus and experts do that," my only goal is to hold up to my end of the deal. That's why I am willing to give you the exact same techniques that I use to grow my passive income revenue streams.

TIME RICH EMPIRE

This offer is not going to be available forever, I have only decided to offer it for a limited time. At first, I was a bit skeptical about giving away the techniques that I used to create a multi million-dollar brand. However, a deal is a deal "I made you a promise and now I am going to hold up to my end of the bargain."

I need you to also pull the trigger and take action, act on this offer now.

<u>**Time Rich Empire - Passive Income Secrets "Step-by-Step Scale Funnel System" Guide To Increase Earnings 50X**</u>

<u>https://timerichempire.com/scale-funnel-system</u>

www.ingramcontent.com/pod-product-compliance
Lightning Source LLC
Chambersburg PA
CBHW031556210526
45464CB00003B/1316